The contents in this journal are of great importance to me; therefore, if you find this, please return it to me. Thank you.

Journal Belongs to

ADDRESS

PHONE NUMBER

Goal-Setting Journal

The book of the life of

_____

Irene Neeposh

iUniverse, Inc.
Bloomington

Goal Setting Journal

iUniverse books may be ordered through booksellers or by contacting:

iUniverse
1663 Liberty Drive
Bloomington, IN 47403
www.iuniverse.com
1-800-Authors (1-800-288-4677)

ISBN: 978-1-4697-8744-2 (sc)
ISBN: 978-1-4697-8745-9 (e)

Printed in the United States of America

iUniverse rev. date: 05/25/2012

To my friend and spiritual mentor Barbara who has being my reminder of where true strength comes from. My Sister Caroline who believed in me without hesitation and to my other siblings, Barbara, Derrick, Peter, and Kim for bringing me the healing power of Laughter and a sense of belonging. To my partner Jonathan, who has continuously pushed me to move forward. To my remarkable mother Ella who has shown me unconditional love and most importantly, to my children Keri-Ann, Isaiah and William who are for me the radiance of God's Merciful love.
Thank you.
With all that I am,

Irene

Table of Contents

Introduction

Reveal your life's dreams—live with a constant awareness and belief that you are working toward making your dreams come true.

Goal setting is a powerful process for mapping your ideal future and for inspiring yourself to turn this vision of the future into a reality.

The process helps you decide what you want in life. By knowing precisely what you want to achieve, you are then empowered to concentrate your efforts. You'll also quickly spot the distractions that waste your time.

As you progressively achieve your goals, and from the clarity of what you have mapped out, you will find your motivation increases, feeding a drive to continually work on progressing toward ... success!

In using a journal to write out your goals, you allow yourself to recognize whether dreams are truly yours or are from external influences. It allows you to see what steps you need to take, by helping you to organize your time.

As you do this, make sure that the goals you have set are genuinely ones that *you* want to achieve.

Now that you are taking your life off autopilot, and are defining who you are, what you want, and what you need to do, you quite possibly will encounter some resistance from people around you. This is only normal, so do not despair in these times; after all, the people around you are getting to know the new you. Be patient with them. It will be with focus, consistency, and a positive attitude that you will reap the benefits.

As you commence this lifestyle of stability, immediately begin to communicate your goals to family, friends, colleagues, and anyone else who might have influence on your life's journey. Do not underestimate the power of positive thinking. Ask! Believe! And receive! It is the law of attraction you need to exuberate. You will be amazed at how your goals will come into being.

You are the driving force of your life. All the dreams you have hold passion that will allow you to persevere. Know that you cannot please everyone. You have one life to live, and your job is to do your best!

How to Use This Journal

First of all, congratulations! The decisions that you have made that led you to this point in your life are now going to take you into whom you will become. Be true to yourself, as what you radiate is what you will attract.

This journal is designed as a tool to help you

1.   Realize your dreams/goals
2.   Map out the means to achieve your goals
3.   Journal your ongoing progress

Section 1 allows you to list your life goals in categories. In it you will write out, paste photos of, or draw images of your dreams/goals. Your life goals will not be achieved in this year, but rather they will be set and the journey toward achieving them will begin.

Section 2 requires you to then map out what you need to do on a day-to-day basis to progress toward your goals. For each month you will find a checklist and a calendar. On the checklist you will, based on your life goals, identify steps you need to take within the subject month; you will further transfer these steps onto the calendar, where you will see what needs your attention for each day. For the calendar you may find it useful to use a color-coding system by assigning colors to each task. As you progressively achieve any items on your checklist, you will be able to check them off!

Section 3 is what you will use to journal your experiences, challenges, doubts, and victories. This will serve as your reference to discover any patterns that might need to be addressed.

It is important that you remain aware of your attitudes toward your goals, making sure that you hold no doubts. If you should have any doubts, then you might want to rethink the goal itself. It may be an externally influenced goal, or it might just be that you need to further develop other areas of your life first. So it could just mean that it will come later.

Have the discipline to devotedly use your journal for a full year, and you will find that the required focus will set in and the needed discipline for achieving your goals will come more naturally.

Practice makes habit; blooming discipline,
Habit makes ritual; blooming stability,
Ritual makes peace; blooming success,
All of which require focus!

Irene Neeposh

This will become the book of your life for the subject year. So decorate it with your drawings, keep it clean, and make it pleasant!

Section 1—Setting Your Goals

In this section you will categorize/organize your goals. By doing this, you will allow yourself to conceptualize your dreams into measurable goals. So retreat to a quiet place, sit back, and bring forth your dreams. The sky is the limit; there are no right or wrong answers. You might find that some of your goals are far-fetched; don't hold back too soon. All that you express in this section will later be put into small steps in the following section. From there you will be able to determine if your goals are realistic for you. Let us begin!

Life Goals

In this section you will draw, paste an image of, or write out how you see yourself once you retire!

Health Goals

As you list your health goals, take into consideration any medical conditions you might have. If you do have a medical condition, cross-check with your doctor to see how realistic your goal(s) are. Furthermore, you might benefit from the assistance of a trainer or physiotherapist.

GOAL	TARGET DATE

Spiritual Goals

Yup, spiritual goals! You might never have thought of setting goals for this area of your life. However, it is important that it not be underestimated. As you list your goals, you might find these to be the most challenging ones to set, and quite possibly the fewest in number. That is fine. Just make sure to give fair consideration to this aspect of your life. Depending on your spiritual practices, you may find it helpful to discuss your goals with either an elder or a spiritual leader from your church or group.

GOAL	TARGET DATE

Keep thy heart with all diligence; for out of it are the issues of life.
Proverbs 4:23

Financial Goals

With all the pressures of life, finances can be the greatest avenue of stress for many. If this is the case for you, then it is vital that your first goal be to meet with someone who can help you sort out and establish a payment plan to get yourself out of the vicious cycle of debt. The services of a financial counselor or a representative from your bank may be of assistance to you. If you are not in debt and have no major financial problems, you are then ready to dream of what you always wanted to buy for either yourself or anyone else.

GOAL	TARGET DATE

Personal Development Goals

Personal development is what keeps us connected to the world around us. It is what we use to be contributing members of our society. You have something to offer, and by sharing this you sow the opportunity for the circle of life to take place in your life. These may not necessarily be career goals; they may quite simply be hobbies.

GOAL	TARGET DATE

Section 2—Mapping Out Your Journey

As you begin the process of mapping out your journey toward reaching your goals, the following section will provide you with means to focus. You may find following your journal on, probably, a daily basis to be a little bothersome in the beginning; however, the fact that you are taking the time to sit, think, and write out your goals may more than likely mean there has been a sense of unruliness in the direction your life has been going. Your journal will serve as a tool to help you obtain the needed discipline to achieve your goals! If you can stay focused, you will see that apart from seeing your goals coming to reality, you will in this time develop the discipline needed to stay focused on where you need to put your energy

The steps you identify on your checklist should be in accordance with your life goals. It may happen that you have identified more than one step within a month for the same goals. That's fine. And you may have nothing for another goal; that's also fine. This is all part of prioritizing.

Checklist for the Month of _____

- ☐ _____
- ☐ _____
- ☐ _____
- ☐ _____
- ☐ _____
- ☐ _____
- ☐ _____
- ☐ _____
- ☐ _____
- ☐ _____
- ☐ _____
- ☐ _____
- ☐ _____
- ☐ _____
- ☐ _____
- ☐ _____
- ☐ _____
- ☐ _____

Month:

Sun	Mon	Tue	Wed	Thu	Fri	Sat

You might find it more readable if you color-code your activities.

☐ _____   ☐ _____

☐ _____   ☐ _____

☐ _____   ☐ _____

☐ _____   ☐ _____

☐ _____   ☐ _____

☐ _____   ☐ _____

Checklist for the Month of _____

- ☐ _____
- ☐ _____
- ☐ _____
- ☐ _____
- ☐ _____
- ☐ _____
- ☐ _____
- ☐ _____
- ☐ _____
- ☐ _____
- ☐ _____
- ☐ _____
- ☐ _____
- ☐ _____
- ☐ _____
- ☐ _____
- ☐ _____
- ☐ _____

Month:

Sun	Mon	Tue	Wed	Thu	Fri	Sat

You might find it more readable if you color-code your activities.

☐ _____   ☐ _____

☐ _____   ☐ _____

☐ _____   ☐ _____

☐ _____   ☐ _____

☐ _____   ☐ _____

☐ _____   ☐ _____

Checklist for the Month of _____

☐ _____

☐ _____

☐ _____

☐ _____

☐ _____

☐ _____

☐ _____

☐ _____

☐ _____

☐ _____

☐ _____

☐ _____

☐ _____

☐ _____

☐ _____

☐ _____

☐ _____

☐ _____

Month:

Sun	Mon	Tue	Wed	Thu	Fri	Sat

You might find it more readable if you color-code your activities.

☐ _____   ☐ _____

☐ _____   ☐ _____

☐ _____   ☐ _____

☐ _____   ☐ _____

☐ _____   ☐ _____

☐ _____   ☐ _____

Checklist for the Month of _____

☐ _____
☐ _____
☐ _____
☐ _____
☐ _____
☐ _____
☐ _____
☐ _____
☐ _____
☐ _____
☐ _____
☐ _____
☐ _____
☐ _____
☐ _____
☐ _____
☐ _____
☐ _____

Month:

Sun	Mon	Tue	Wed	Thu	Fri	Sat

You might find it more readable if you color-code your activities.

☐ _____   ☐ _____

☐ _____   ☐ _____

☐ _____   ☐ _____

☐ _____   ☐ _____

☐ _____   ☐ _____

☐ _____   ☐ _____

Checklist for the Month of _____

- ☐ _____
- ☐ _____
- ☐ _____
- ☐ _____
- ☐ _____
- ☐ _____
- ☐ _____
- ☐ _____
- ☐ _____
- ☐ _____
- ☐ _____
- ☐ _____
- ☐ _____
- ☐ _____
- ☐ _____
- ☐ _____
- ☐ _____
- ☐ _____

Month:

Sun	Mon	Tue	Wed	Thu	Fri	Sat

You might find it more readable if you color-code your activities.

☐ _____   ☐ _____

☐ _____   ☐ _____

☐ _____   ☐ _____

☐ _____   ☐ _____

☐ _____   ☐ _____

☐ _____   ☐ _____

Checklist for the Month of _____

- [ ] _____
- [ ] _____
- [ ] _____
- [ ] _____
- [ ] _____
- [ ] _____
- [ ] _____
- [ ] _____
- [ ] _____
- [ ] _____
- [ ] _____
- [ ] _____
- [ ] _____
- [ ] _____
- [ ] _____
- [ ] _____
- [ ] _____
- [ ] _____

Month:

Sun	Mon	Tue	Wed	Thu	Fri	Sat

You might find it more readable if you color-code your activities.

☐ _____   ☐ _____

☐ _____   ☐ _____

☐ _____   ☐ _____

☐ _____   ☐ _____

☐ _____   ☐ _____

☐ _____   ☐ _____

Checklist for the Month of _____

- [ ] _____
- [ ] _____
- [ ] _____
- [ ] _____
- [ ] _____
- [ ] _____
- [ ] _____
- [ ] _____
- [ ] _____
- [ ] _____
- [ ] _____
- [ ] _____
- [ ] _____
- [ ] _____
- [ ] _____
- [ ] _____
- [ ] _____
- [ ] _____

Month:

Sun	Mon	Tue	Wed	Thu	Fri	Sat

You might find it more readable if you color-code your activities.

☐ _____   ☐ _____

☐ _____   ☐ _____

☐ _____   ☐ _____

☐ _____   ☐ _____

☐ _____   ☐ _____

☐ _____   ☐ _____

Checklist for the Month of _____

- ☐ _____
- ☐ _____
- ☐ _____
- ☐ _____
- ☐ _____
- ☐ _____
- ☐ _____
- ☐ _____
- ☐ _____
- ☐ _____
- ☐ _____
- ☐ _____
- ☐ _____
- ☐ _____
- ☐ _____
- ☐ _____
- ☐ _____
- ☐ _____

Month:

Sun	Mon	Tue	Wed	Thu	Fri	Sat

You might find it more readable if you color-code your activities.

☐ _____   ☐ _____

☐ _____   ☐ _____

☐ _____   ☐ _____

☐ _____   ☐ _____

☐ _____   ☐ _____

☐ _____   ☐ _____

Checklist for the Month of _____

☐ _____

☐ _____

☐ _____

☐ _____

☐ _____

☐ _____

☐ _____

☐ _____

☐ _____

☐ _____

☐ _____

☐ _____

☐ _____

☐ _____

☐ _____

☐ _____

☐ _____

☐ _____

Month:

Sun	Mon	Tue	Wed	Thu	Fri	Sat

You might find it more readable if you color-code your activities.

☐ _____   ☐ _____

☐ _____   ☐ _____

☐ _____   ☐ _____

☐ _____   ☐ _____

☐ _____   ☐ _____

☐ _____   ☐ _____

Checklist for the Month of _____

- ☐ _____
- ☐ _____
- ☐ _____
- ☐ _____
- ☐ _____
- ☐ _____
- ☐ _____
- ☐ _____
- ☐ _____
- ☐ _____
- ☐ _____
- ☐ _____
- ☐ _____
- ☐ _____
- ☐ _____
- ☐ _____
- ☐ _____
- ☐ _____

Month:

Sun	Mon	Tue	Wed	Thu	Fri	Sat

You might find it more readable if you color-code your activities.

☐ _____   ☐ _____

☐ _____   ☐ _____

☐ _____   ☐ _____

☐ _____   ☐ _____

☐ _____   ☐ _____

☐ _____   ☐ _____

Checklist for the Month of _____

☐ _____

☐ _____

☐ _____

☐ _____

☐ _____

☐ _____

☐ _____

☐ _____

☐ _____

☐ _____

☐ _____

☐ _____

☐ _____

☐ _____

☐ _____

☐ _____

☐ _____

☐ _____

Month:

Sun	Mon	Tue	Wed	Thu	Fri	Sat

You might find it more readable if you color-code your activities.

☐ _____   ☐ _____

☐ _____   ☐ _____

☐ _____   ☐ _____

☐ _____   ☐ _____

☐ _____   ☐ _____

☐ _____   ☐ _____

Checklist for the Month of _____

- ☐ _____
- ☐ _____
- ☐ _____
- ☐ _____
- ☐ _____
- ☐ _____
- ☐ _____
- ☐ _____
- ☐ _____
- ☐ _____
- ☐ _____
- ☐ _____
- ☐ _____
- ☐ _____
- ☐ _____
- ☐ _____
- ☐ _____
- ☐ _____

Month:

Sun	Mon	Tue	Wed	Thu	Fri	Sat

You might find it more readable if you color-code your activities.

☐ _____   ☐ _____

☐ _____   ☐ _____

☐ _____   ☐ _____

☐ _____   ☐ _____

☐ _____   ☐ _____

☐ _____   ☐ _____

Section 3—Journal Entries

DATE:

DATE: _____

_____
_____
_____
_____
_____
_____
_____
_____
_____
_____
_____
_____
_____
_____
_____
_____
_____
_____
_____
_____
_____
_____
_____
_____
_____
_____
_____

DATE:

DATE:

DATE:

DATE: _____

_____
_____
_____
_____
_____
_____
_____
_____
_____
_____
_____
_____
_____
_____
_____
_____
_____
_____
_____
_____
_____
_____
_____
_____
_____
_____

DATE:

DATE: _____

DATE: _____

_____
_____
_____
_____
_____
_____
_____
_____
_____
_____
_____
_____
_____
_____
_____
_____
_____
_____
_____
_____
_____
_____
_____
_____
_____
_____
_____
_____
_____

DATE:

DATE:

DATE:

DATE:

DATE:

DATE:

47

DATE:

DATE: _____

_____
_____
_____
_____
_____
_____
_____
_____
_____
_____
_____
_____
_____
_____
_____
_____
_____
_____
_____
_____
_____
_____
_____
_____
_____
_____
_____

DATE: _____

_____
_____
_____
_____
_____
_____
_____
_____
_____
_____
_____
_____
_____
_____
_____
_____
_____
_____
_____
_____
_____
_____
_____
_____
_____
_____
_____
_____

DATE:

DATE:

DATE:

DATE:

DATE:

Irene sees the challenges that people face. After running for Chief in her Native Community of Waswanipi, Quebec she returned to school to further her education in Business Development as she strongly believes in economic development. Through all the dynamic changes in her life, she continues to work with people in overcoming setback and believes that each person has the power to be all that they want to be.